Enriched Love

Calotta D. Porterfield

Published by
GWW Publishing
www.gwwpublishing.com

Providing Publishing Services for Christian Authors & Organizations: Hardbacks, Paperbacks, E-Books & Audiobooks.

Enriched Love

Copyright © 2018 by CALOTTA D. Porterfield.

All rights reserved.

This book is protected by copyright laws of the United States of America. The author guarantees the contents are original and do not infringe upon the legal rights of any other person or work. NO part of this book may be reproduced in any form without the permission of the author. The views expressed in this book are not necessarily those of the publisher.

ISBN-13: 978-1-948829-00-7

Printed in the United States of America

First Edition: February 2018

DEDICATION

I dedicate this book in loving memory of my mother Minster Ruby McKever Floyd who left a legacy of the importance of uninterrupted "quiet time" spent with and before God.

Table Of Contents

Chapter 1: Where Are You Spending Your Time?   *3*

Chapter 2: You Do Have Enough Time   *7*

Chapter 3: Busy or Productive   *11*

Chapter 4: When I AM is With Us, We Have Enriched Love   *14*

Closing Thoughts   *17*

Enriched Love Workbook   *20*

About the Author   *86*

Introduction

There was a time when you ordered coffee and the following were flavors: original cream-powder, sugar, decaf, caffeine or black. Today, there are more flavor choices such as caramel, hazelnut, vanilla, French vanilla, honey, coffee served with ice and so much more. Depending on a person's involvement: every day actions, home chores, school or church activities, community services, committee participation, homeowners association duties, sorority and fraternity functions, and let's not forget, sporting events! It's no wonder we find ourselves implying that more time is needed in a day.

No matter how busy we are, there is a deep need to pull away for quiet time with God. A quiet time that allows God to refresh, refocus, and enrich our relationship with Him. There is a need to free our lives of interruptions because time is so precious and is often a challenge by our *many flavored* schedules.

Enriched Love focuses on bringing awareness to how we have not managed our time to include God; versus understanding the importance for managing our time to increase our relationship with God, so that He can enrich us spiritually to experience His love and all that He provides. We sometimes spend our lives on "time wasters" instead of trying to eliminate them or at the least avoiding the distractions. *Enriched Love* will require the need to distinguish between busy and productive time, understanding wholeheartedly what it really means to have quiet time with God.

Upon completion of reading this book, a workbook has been included to assist you in developing a personal plan and set a goal that includes daily time with God, so that He can lead you to His *Enriched Love*.

Chapter 1

Where are you spending your time?

In the past, week after week, situations and conversations left me asking this question, "WHERE ARE YOU SPENDING YOUR TIME?"

James 4:14 NLT tells us, "How do you know what your life will be like tomorrow? Your life is like the morning fog- it's here a little while, then it's gone."

The Epistle of James was written in a time when death was imminent, a time of great persecution of believers, because of their faith in Jesus Christ. The trials the first century church faced was a daily reminder of a real sacrifice, because of an eternal choice, following Christ. Is this still true for the body of Christ today? Are we concerned about the souls of others, or are we distracted with obtaining earthly acclaim? Do we share the love of Christ truly with everyone in the way we live daily? Do we just shine light on other Christians during the two to three hours we spend in our houses of worship?

Do we get up with an expectation to live a self-LESS life? Are our personal agendas and motives more important than the wellbeing of others? The Apostle James in James 4:14 asked a powerful question, "How do you know what your life will be like tomorrow?" Do we know where we will be from one second to an hour to the next? Will we be physically strong or weak? Up or down? In our right minds or living with no sense of reality? Will we be able to care for ourselves or depending on the generosity of others?

We do not have all the answers to these questions, or even the question posed by the Apostle James. Nevertheless, there is someone who does and we must take time to spend with Him to listen and hear. We must act and live in such away, as I can remember my Mom saying "To live your life in such a way as if today was your last." Every interaction should be intentional and godly impactful.

It is time to live a life that GIVES, one that fosters LOVE when others encounter it. We must make the TIME, give a

COUNT meaning we must consider if we are truly fulfilling our God-given purpose on the earth. We must seek to truly come to a realization of what God would have us to spend time on in every area of our lives. If our business has been self-gratification, it is time to hang up the GOING OUT OF BUSINESS sign, due to NEW MANAGEMENT!

Jesus stated when he was twelve, "That He must be about His Father's business," yet for a season He submitted Himself to His earthly parents and in Luke 2:52 NASB a beautiful commentary of this time of maturation was given, "**And Jesus kept increasing in wisdom and stature, and in favor with God and men.**"

We too are so deserving of an increase in wisdom and stature in favor with God and men. In our lives, we go through seasons of maturation where there should be only an increase of wisdom; but also of TIME.

Time is needed and should be spent in productive interaction and not distractive meaningless actions. God has not called us to WASTE time, but to be GOOD STEWARDS OF TIME.

Chapter 2

You do have enough time

Have you ever said this, "I do not have enough time!"? Have you ever started your day and looked up and it was time to go home? Have you ever prayed for 24 more hours? Well, 24 hours is all we are going to receive. Consider the following quote from the late Pastor Adrian Rogers:

"Each new day brings us 24 hours, 1440 minutes, 86 seconds, each moment a precious gift from God. We face the future out of breath, because we have been fighting tomorrow's battles today."

Matthew 7:34b (NKJV) reminds us that "Sufficient is for the day is its own trouble." Every person on earth that wakes up is given the same amount of hours in a day; therefore, the problem is not the time but how we personally chose to REDEEM it.

The Word of God through the voice of the Apostle Paul instructs us to "Redeem the time." Hmmm… just what does that mean to "redeem the time"?

Ephesians 5:15, 16 (NKJV) states:

"See then that you walk circumspectly, not as fools but as wise, REDEEMING THE TIME, because the days are evil"

The time in this scripture is referring to "redeeming opportunities." The Greek word "kairos" means "a fixed or definite period of time which something can be accomplished that cannot be accomplished after the time has passed."

Live in the moment; praying in the present; adoring God NOW!

The word *redeem* in Ephesians 5:15 means to "buy out of the marketplace." Therefore, picture yourself in your favorite retail store. After walking through the door, you realize the "**on sale**" signs all over the store. You immediately slowed down, (taking the time) to look through each rack, carefully selecting items with the best bargains. With such an example, understand that you *redeem the time*, making it a necessity to bargain shop due to the "**on sale**" signs. Seizing the opportunity to bargain shop is not nearly as important as it is to "seize the opportunity to *make time*" for God.

If we fail to realize that time not spent with God daily, disallows us to grow spiritually. Then accomplishing goals and tasks that are imperative for our purpose in the marketplace, become irrelevant. We are living each day as a busy person. **There is ALWAYS time for God!** If you want to fulfill your God given purpose in life, then you will make time for God.

It is imperative to walk (live) each day being alert to the opportunities that God has placed in the "marketplace" to help us be productive. The MARKETPLACE is the world in which we live! It is our home, work, community and church or as I like to say, "Where we worship." God has assigned a specific time on earth called LIFE. We have opportunities to share and illustrate Him in the earth. Therefore, we must carefully examine daily interaction, as we do items in a store on sale, and maximize the time we have been given, making time for God.

Chapter 3

Busy or Productive

While thinking of a plain way to illustrate how our being busy affects our ability to enrich our relationship with God, He literally showed me this.

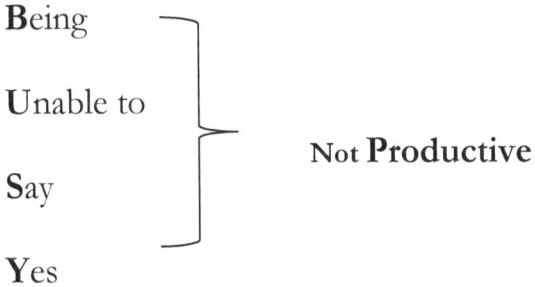

Being

Unable to

Say

Yes
} **Not Productive**

Is that not powerful? Stop, examine your schedule in a 24-hour period and ask, "What AM I B.U.S.Y. Doing? I have experienced times when I have overcommitted to things (events, appointments, opportunities, etc.) that I knew deep inside were not productive. Yes, they could have been what might be described by others as "good things" and even "ministry." However, here is the *litmus test* …are the good things, ministry coming before your ability to enrich the love relationship with the One who created you? I realized that I was doing what "I thought" God would have me doing without first consulting Him. We **must** check to see what *HIS* plan is for us.

Our personal agendas prevent us from saying, "yes" to God's true purpose for our lives. **B**eing **U**nable to **S**ay **Y**es may even delay what I believe is God's best for us, because He will not override our decisions. When we over commit ourselves, it leaves no time to commit to God and His designed plan for us. Leaving plenty room for us to miss the mark or our season.

This brings to mind one of many scriptures that empowered me to start managing my time, and notice I said, "start" because I can still get distracted.

John replied, "No one can receive anything unless God gives it from heaven."

John 3:27 (NLT)

When I need true direction, I have learned and still learning to intentionally schedule time **with** God. If you notice, I did not say **for** because He is always there for us, but we have to make a decision to stop and be present with Him. John 3:27 shifted my personal reaction to God's answers to my prayers during quiet time. I came to a true realization of the enriched love in my relationship with Him. The God that made me and knows everything about me, answers me from heaven and not just me, but YOU TOO. When we accept a relationship with HIM that is what He wants, desires, and created humankind to enjoy with Him. To be ENRICHED with His LOVE.

· Chapter 4 ·

When I AM is with us, we have Enriched Love

We as humans concentrate on the quantity of time before we consider the quality of time. I remember as a new believer listening to all the believers speak about how much time they spent with God and how they got up early in the morning to meet Him. I would work so hard to do the same thing I heard and to copy their pattern. Only to find myself discouraged, empty, and feeling guilty.

I learned as I sought God personally, that we are not to feel guilty but enriched from setting aside time to seek His love and instruction. The desire to spend time with God in enriching our relationship with Him should not be motivated out of guilt, but out of a love for Him.

"So now, there is no condemnation for those who belong to Christ Jesus"

Romans 8:1 (NLT)

In its context, this scripture is speaking of our freedom from sin and death when we enter into a relationship with God through Christ Jesus. Here I shared it, because God reminded me and I want to encourage **you**; that God's love and our desire to be with Him would not produce discouragement, emptiness or guilt. He has empowered us to make the decision at any time during the 24 hours to have time with Him, whether in the morning, midday or all day, His ENRICHED LOVE is readily available.

We see that very example in Luke 5:16 (NLT) when He describes how Jesus manages quiet time while on earth.

"But Jesus often withdrew to lonely places to pray."

When I AM is with us, we have ENRICHED LOVE. The place does not matter, because we have been empowered to manage our day. When I AM is with us, He answers us from heaven, His throne. We have been empowered to pull up and seek His guidance and direction, whether at home, work, or driving alone in the car.

God loves us so much that He put on flesh, was born, lived, died and *rose for us*. We need only to accept His love and to take time for our love to become ENRICHED LOVE.

CLOSING THOUGHTS

We have to now admit that being **B.U.S.Y.** is not an indication that one is necessarily productive. So how do we move from Being Unable to Say Yes to productive and have ENRICHED LOVE? It starts with a decision followed by actions to manage the gift of time that God has provided.

Remember, we have been and are empowered through our relationship with God to make the choice to put Him first. But how? I am glad you asked. Allow me to share from a personal list ways to walk this out.

1. *Plan your quiet time*

    You have the power to schedule time in your day with God and to hear from Him.

2. *Write down appointments, meetings, and events in pencil*

    Filling out your calendar with a pencil gives you the power to change your mind and manage the gift of time that God has given you.

3. ***Keep personal and business dates on one calendar***

    Having all dates in one place empowers your ability to be a steward of where and how you spend your time. No white space equals no time for purpose. Avoid being **B.U.S.Y.**

4. ***Identify your peak times***

    Spend time with God when you are at your best. For some that is early in the morning and for others it is late at night.

5. ***Say "No" without why***

    Having to explain your choice to others gives them power. Remember, you have been empowered from Heaven to manage the gift of time.

6. ***Become comfortable with silence***

    God will not compete for our attention, so learn to sit in silence so you can train your ears to hear.

7. ***Give up the need "TO DO"***

    Always having the need "TO DO", it is an indication that your inner man is not at rest. Trust will require our surrender.

8. ***Drive in silence***

    Make your car an "altar" no phone, no radio. Enjoy God's creation instead.

9. ***Go to lunch alone sometime***

    This is a daily gift to sit quietly.

10. ***Have another day of Rest***

    Sunday for some is a ministry workday, so schedule another day to truly rest. No appointments, no commitments and no phone.

Enriched Love

Workbook

Introduction

The **Enriched Love** workbook will provide a 21-day journey, where you are encouraged to schedule time for intimacy with God through daily observation of selected scriptures. Each scripture chosen is to ENRICH, INSPIRE and MOTIVATE your life.

The journey begins with a self-examination of where you are personally spending the 24 hours given to all of us for each day. The self-examination is then followed by three areas of commitment:

- ❖ Commitment to TIME

- ❖ Commitment to LOVE

- ❖ Commitment to CULTIVATION

Why you ask? We sense that our lives are out of sync. We often describe it as being "out of balance". Our schedules are full with activities that do not add to or fulfill purpose. As stated earlier, we must make sure we are not B.U.S.Y (Being Unable to Say Yes), but productive. How we manage our time says a lot about how much we value the purpose of God in our lives.

The ultimate goal of this workbook is to create a habit of setting aside time that will be an integral part of your daily life.

Where Does the Time Go?

TIME is the most important element of any relationship. If we were to ask couples that have spent years or even decades together to give advice on what makes a relationship intimate, we would find TIME at the top of the list. It is hard to be in any relationship and not spend quality time. When time is spent together, love is cultivated, dreams are shared, joys are developed and trials are put into perspective.

Our relationship with God should not be any different. Time spent is not wasted or empty but FULL. ENRICHED LOVE brings about a peace that cannot be explained.

... *time spent is not wasted or empty, but FULL.*

What does it take to experience ERICHED LOVE? It takes COMMITMENT to:

- ❖ TIME

- ❖ Your LOVE and CULTIVATION.

Time is expensive, spend it well

The first step to ENRICHED LOVE is to ask: **Where am I spending my TIME?**

In order to answer this question, on the next page look at your life Monday thru Sunday, record what you are doing by the corresponding hour(s). After recording your activities, complete the **Post Review** questions by recording what you have learned by answering the four question provided.

Example: recording of day time

	Monday
12 am - 1am	sleep
2am - 3am	sleep
4am - 5am	sleep
6am - 7am	Wake/get ready for work
8am - 9am	In car to work/at work
10am - 11am	Check emails/conference call
11am - 12pm	Respond to emails/calls
1pm-2pm	lunch
3pm- 4pm	Team conference call

Note: I did not include normal sleeping hours.

	Monday
4:00 AM	
5:00 AM	
6:00 AM	
7:00 AM	
8:00 AM	
9:00 AM	
10:00 AM	
11:00 AM	
12:00 PM	
1:00 PM	
2:00 PM	
3:00 PM	
4:00 PM	

5:00 PM	
6:00 PM	
7:00 PM	
8:00 PM	
9:00 PM	
10:00 PM	
11:00 PM	
12:00 AM	

Notes:

_____

_____

_____

_____

_____

_____

	Tuesday
4:00 AM	
5:00 AM	
6:00 AM	
7:00 AM	
8:00 AM	
9:00 AM	
10:00 AM	
11:00 AM	
12:00 PM	
1:00 PM	
2:00 PM	
3:00 PM	
4:00 PM	
5:00 PM	

6:00 PM	
7:00 PM	
8:00 PM	
9:00 PM	
10:00 PM	
11:00 PM	
12:00 AM	

Notes:

_____

_____

_____

_____

_____

_____

_____

	Wednesday
4:00 AM	
5:00 AM	
6:00 AM	
7:00 AM	
8:00 AM	
9:00 AM	
10:00 AM	
11:00 AM	
12:00 PM	
1:00 PM	
2:00 PM	
3:00 PM	
4:00 PM	
5:00 PM	

6:00 PM	
7:00 PM	
8:00 PM	
9:00 PM	
10:00 PM	
11:00 PM	
12:00 AM	

Notes:

_____

_____

_____

_____

_____

_____

_____

	Thursday
4:00 AM	
5:00 AM	
6:00 AM	
7:00 AM	
8:00 AM	
9:00 AM	
10:00 AM	
11:00 AM	
12:00 PM	
1:00 PM	
2:00 PM	
3:00 PM	
4:00 PM	
5:00 PM	

6:00 PM	
7:00 PM	
8:00 PM	
9:00 PM	
10:00 PM	
11:00 PM	
12:00 AM	

Notes:

_____

_____

_____

_____

_____

_____

_____

	Friday
4:00 AM	
5:00 AM	
6:00 AM	
7:00 AM	
8:00 AM	
9:00 AM	
10:00 AM	
11:00 AM	
12:00 PM	
1:00 PM	
2:00 PM	
3:00 PM	
4:00 PM	
5:00 PM	

6:00 PM	
7:00 PM	
8:00 PM	
9:00 PM	
10:00 PM	
11:00 PM	
12:00 AM	

Notes:

_____

_____

_____

_____

_____

_____

_____

	Saturday
4:00 AM	
5:00 AM	
6:00 AM	
7:00 AM	
8:00 AM	
9:00 AM	
10:00 AM	
11:00 AM	
12:00 PM	
1:00 PM	
2:00 PM	
3:00 PM	
4:00 PM	
5:00 PM	

6:00 PM	
7:00 PM	
8:00 PM	
9:00 PM	
10:00 PM	
11:00 PM	
12:00 AM	

Notes:

_____

_____

_____

_____

_____

_____

_____

	Sunday
4:00 AM	
5:00 AM	
6:00 AM	
7:00 AM	
8:00 AM	
9:00 AM	
10:00 AM	
11:00 AM	
12:00 PM	
1:00 PM	
2:00 PM	
3:00 PM	
4:00 PM	
5:00 PM	

6:00 PM	
7:00 PM	
8:00 PM	
9:00 PM	
10:00 PM	
11:00 PM	
12:00 AM	

Notes:

_____

_____

_____

_____

_____

_____

_____

SELF-EXAMINATION POST REVIEW QUESTIONS

"God will not work within the framework of our complicated schedules; we must adapt to His style.[1]"

1. Most of my time is spent:

_____

_____

_____

_____

_____

_____

_____

_____

_____

_____

[1] Swindoll, C. (2007). *So, You Want To Be Like Christ?: Eight Essentials to Get You There.* Nelson Publishing

2. What activities can I delegate or stop altogether?

_____

_____

_____

_____

_____

_____

3. Did you have any time sitting quietly? Why or why not?

_____

_____

_____

_____

_____

_____

4. What will you do differently? Why or why not?

Commitment to Time

In a relationship no one wants to be alone. Often we judge the success of our relationships on the quantity of time spent. God's love is the same. It demands and calls for our time. The Word of God tells us, *"He chose us in Him before the foundation of the world, that we should be holy and blameless before Him in love." (Ephesians 1:4 NASB).* He desires time with us.

For the remainder of this workbook we will provide scriptures that will encourage and assist you in strengthening the three commitment mentioned earlier.

- ❖ Commitment to TIME
- ❖ Commitment to LOVE
- ❖ Commitment to CULTIVATION

Instructions:

- ❖ Start with 5 minutes each day for the next 21 days to read scriptures provided related to the 3 commitments:

    1. Commitment to TIME - Day 1 thru Day 7

    2. Commitment to LOVE - Day 8 thru Day 15

    3. Commitment to CULTIVATE - Day 16 thru Day 21

- ❖ Record your personal reaction to the scripture and how you will apply to your life

- ❖ Lastly, write out a prayer of communication to God

DAY 1

Psalm 90:12 (NKJV)
So teach us to number our days, that we may gain a heart of wisdom

Personal Observations:

_____
_____
_____
_____
_____
_____
_____

Personal Application:

_____
_____
_____
_____
_____
_____
_____

Prayer of Communication:

DAY 2

Ephesians 5:16-17 (ESV)
Look carefully then how you walk, not as unwise but as wise, making the best use of the time, because the days are evil. Therefore do not be foolish, but understand what the will of the Lord is.

Personal Observations:

_____
_____
_____
_____
_____
_____
_____

Personal Application:

_____
_____
_____
_____
_____
_____
_____

Prayer of Communication:

DAY 3

Proverbs 16:9 (NKJV)
A man's heart plans his way, But the LORD directs his steps.

Personal Observations:

_____
_____
_____
_____
_____
_____
_____

Personal Application:

_____
_____
_____
_____
_____
_____

Prayer of Communication:

DAY 4

James 4:14-15 (NKJV)

whereas you do not know what will happen tomorrow. For what is your life? It is even a vapor that appears for a little time and then vanishes away. Instead you ought to say, "If the Lord wills, we shall live and do this or that."

Personal Observations:

_____

_____

_____

_____

_____

_____

_____

Personal Application:

_____

_____

_____

_____

_____

_____

Prayer of Communication:

DAY 5

2 Peter 3:8 (NKJV)
But, beloved, do not forget this one thing, that with the Lord one day is as a thousand years, and a thousand years as one day

Personal Observations:

_____
_____
_____
_____
_____
_____
_____

Personal Application:

_____
_____
_____
_____
_____
_____

Prayer of Communication:

DAY 6

Proverbs 16:3 (ESV)
Commit your work to the LORD, and your plans will be established.

Personal Observations:

_____
_____
_____
_____
_____
_____
_____

Personal Application:

_____
_____
_____
_____
_____
_____
_____

Prayer of Communication:

DAY 7

Jeremiah 29:11 (NLT)
*For I know the plans I have for you," says the L*ORD*. "They are plans for good and not for disaster, to give you a future and a hope.*

Personal Observations:

_____
_____
_____
_____
_____
_____
_____

Personal Application:

_____
_____
_____
_____
_____
_____

Prayer of Communication:

DAY 8

Deuteronomy 6:5 (KJV)
And thou shalt love the Lord they God with all thine heart, and with all thy soul, and with all thy might

Personal Observations:

_____
_____
_____
_____
_____
_____
_____

Personal Application:

_____
_____
_____
_____
_____
_____

Prayer of Communication:

DAY 9

Proverbs 145:20 (ESV)
The LORD preserves all who love him, but all the wicked he will destroy

Personal Observations:

_____
_____
_____
_____
_____
_____
_____

Personal Application:

_____
_____
_____
_____
_____
_____

Prayer of Communication:

DAY 10

Leviticus 26:12 (ESV)
And I will walk among you and will be your God, and you shall be my people.

Personal Observations:

_____
_____
_____
_____
_____
_____
_____

Personal Application:

_____
_____
_____
_____
_____
_____
_____

Prayer of Communication:

DAY 11

John 15:4 (ESV)
Abide in me, and I in you. As the branch cannot bear fruit by itself, unless it abides in the vine, neither can you, unless you abide in me.

Personal Observations:

_____
_____
_____
_____
_____
_____
_____

Personal Application:

_____
_____
_____
_____
_____
_____

Prayer of Communication:

DAY 12

Psalm 91:14 (KJV)
Because he hath set his love upon me, therefore will I deliver him;
I will set him on high , because he hath known my name.

Personal Observations:

_____
_____
_____
_____
_____
_____

Personal Application:

_____
_____
_____
_____
_____
_____

Prayer of Communication:

DAY 13

Proverbs 8:17 (ESV)
I love those who love me, and those who seek me diligently find me.

Personal Observations:

_____
_____
_____
_____
_____
_____
_____

Personal Application:

_____
_____
_____
_____
_____
_____
_____

Prayer of Communication:

DAY 14

2 Thessalonians 3:5 (ESV)
May the Lord direct your hearts to the love of God and to the steadfastness of Christ.

Personal Observations:

_____
_____
_____
_____
_____
_____
_____

Personal Application:

_____
_____
_____
_____
_____
_____

Prayer of Communication:

DAY 15

Romans 12:1 (NASB)
Therefore I urge you, brethren, by the mercies of God, to present your bodies a living and holy sacrifice, acceptable to God which is your spiritual service of worship.

Personal Observations:

_____
_____
_____
_____
_____
_____
_____

Personal Application:

_____
_____
_____
_____
_____
_____
_____

Prayer of Communication:

DAY 16

Hebrews 13:15 (NKJV)
Therefore by Him let us continually offer the sacrifice of praise to God, that is, the fruit of our lips, giving thanks to His name.

Personal Observations:

_____
_____
_____
_____
_____
_____
_____

Personal Application:

_____
_____
_____
_____
_____
_____

Prayer of Communication:

DAY 17

Ephesians 4:17 (NKJV)
This I say, therefore, and testify in the Lord, that you should no longer walk as the rest of the Gentiles walk, in the futility of their mind

Personal Observations:

_____
_____
_____
_____
_____
_____
_____

Personal Application:

_____
_____
_____
_____
_____
_____
_____

Prayer of Communication:

DAY 18

Psalm 119:15-16 (ESV)
I will meditate on your precepts and fix my eyes on your ways. I will delight in your statutes; I will not forget your word.

Personal Observations:

_____
_____
_____
_____
_____
_____

Personal Application:

_____
_____
_____
_____
_____
_____

Prayer of Communication:

DAY 19

2 Chronicles 7:14 (ESV)
if my people who are called by my name humble themselves, and pray and seek my face and turn from their wicked ways, then I will hear from heaven and will forgive their sin and heal their land.

Personal Observations:

_____
_____
_____
_____
_____
_____
_____

Personal Application:

_____
_____
_____
_____
_____
_____

Prayer of Communication:

DAY 20

Luke 10:42 (NKJV)
But one thing is needed, and Mary has chosen that good part, which will not be taken away from her."

Personal Observations:

_____
_____
_____
_____
_____
_____
_____

Personal Application:

_____
_____
_____
_____
_____
_____
_____

Prayer of Communication:

DAY 21

1 Chronicles 16:11 (NKJV)
Seek the Lord and His strength; Seek His face evermore!

Personal Observations:

_____
_____
_____
_____
_____
_____

Personal Application:

_____
_____
_____
_____
_____

Prayer of Communication:

ABOUT THE AUTHOR

Calotta is a servant unto God and His people, possessing a teaching and preaching ministry that stresses the importance of having a personal and intimate relationship with God through the love and application of His word. Out of this love, God is birthing **D.I.V.E. (Define, Investigate, Verify, and Engage)** which is dedicated to enriching lives in truth through small group discussions, one on one mentoring and media.

One of her many favorite scriptures is 2 Timothy 2:15 *"Study to shew thyself approved unto God, A workman that needeth not to be ashamed rightly dividing the word of truth."*